ROYAL HORTICULTURAL SOCIETY

WILD IN THE
GARDEN
DIARY
2025

First published in 2024 by Frances Lincoln Publishing,
an imprint of The Quarto Group.
One Triptych Place, London, SE1 9SH, United Kingdom
www.Quarto.com

A catalogue record for this book is available from the
British Library.

ISBN 978-0-7112-9184-3

10 9 8 7 6 5 4 3 2 1

Printed in China

RHS FLOWER SHOWS 2025
The Royal Horticultural Society holds a number of
prestigious flower shows throughout the year. At the time
of going to press, show dates for 2025 had not been
confirmed but details can be found on the website at:
rhs.org.uk/shows-events

Every effort is made to ensure calendarial data is correct
at the time of going to press but the publisher cannot
accept any liability for any errors or changes.

Front cover: Common dormouse (*Muscardinus
avellanarius*)
Back cover: 7-spot ladybird (*Coccinella septempunctata*)
First page: Birdhouse with great tit (*Parus major*)

CALENDAR 2025

JANUARY
M	T	W	T	F	S	S
		1	2	3	4	5
6	7	8	9	10	11	12
13	14	15	16	17	18	19
20	21	22	23	24	25	26
27	28	29	30	31		

FEBRUARY
M	T	W	T	F	S	S
					1	2
3	4	5	6	7	8	9
10	11	12	13	14	15	16
17	18	19	20	21	22	23
24	25	26	27	28		

MARCH
M	T	W	T	F	S	S
					1	2
3	4	5	6	7	8	9
10	11	12	13	14	15	16
17	18	19	20	21	22	23
24	25	26	27	28	29	30
31						

APRIL
M	T	W	T	F	S	S
	1	2	3	4	5	6
7	8	9	10	11	12	13
14	15	16	17	18	19	20
21	22	23	24	25	26	27
28	29	30				

MAY
M	T	W	T	F	S	S
			1	2	3	4
5	6	7	8	9	10	11
12	13	14	15	16	17	18
19	20	21	22	23	24	25
26	27	28	29	30	31	

JUNE
M	T	W	T	F	S	S
						1
2	3	4	5	6	7	8
9	10	11	12	13	14	15
16	17	18	19	20	21	22
23	24	25	26	27	28	29
30						

JULY
M	T	W	T	F	S	S
	1	2	3	4	5	6
7	8	9	10	11	12	13
14	15	16	17	18	19	20
21	22	23	24	25	26	27
28	29	30	31			

AUGUST
M	T	W	T	F	S	S
				1	2	3
4	5	6	7	8	9	10
11	12	13	14	15	16	17
18	19	20	21	22	23	24
25	26	27	28	29	30	31

SEPTEMBER
M	T	W	T	F	S	S
1	2	3	4	5	6	7
8	9	10	11	12	13	14
15	16	17	18	19	20	21
22	23	24	25	26	27	28
29	30					

OCTOBER
M	T	W	T	F	S	S
		1	2	3	4	5
6	7	8	9	10	11	12
13	14	15	16	17	18	19
20	21	22	23	24	25	26
27	28	29	30	31		

NOVEMBER
M	T	W	T	F	S	S
					1	2
3	4	5	6	7	8	9
10	11	12	13	14	15	16
17	18	19	20	21	22	23
24	25	26	27	28	29	30

DECEMBER
M	T	W	T	F	S	S
1	2	3	4	5	6	7
8	9	10	11	12	13	14
15	16	17	18	19	20	21
22	23	24	25	26	27	28
29	30	31				

CALENDAR 2026

JANUARY
M	T	W	T	F	S	S
			1	2	3	4
5	6	7	8	9	10	11
12	13	14	15	16	17	18
19	20	21	22	23	24	25
26	27	28	29	30	31	

FEBRUARY
M	T	W	T	F	S	S
						1
2	3	4	5	6	7	8
9	10	11	12	13	14	15
16	17	18	19	20	21	22
23	24	25	26	27	28	

MARCH
M	T	W	T	F	S	S
						1
2	3	4	5	6	7	8
9	10	11	12	13	14	15
16	17	18	19	20	21	22
23	24	25	26	27	28	29
30	31					

APRIL
M	T	W	T	F	S	S
		1	2	3	4	5
6	7	8	9	10	11	12
13	14	15	16	17	18	19
20	21	22	23	24	25	26
27	28	29	30			

MAY
M	T	W	T	F	S	S
				1	2	3
4	5	6	7	8	9	10
11	12	13	14	15	16	17
18	19	20	21	22	23	24
25	26	27	28	29	30	31

JUNE
M	T	W	T	F	S	S
1	2	3	4	5	6	7
8	9	10	11	12	13	14
15	16	17	18	19	20	21
22	23	24	25	26	27	28
29	30					

JULY
M	T	W	T	F	S	S
		1	2	3	4	5
6	7	8	9	10	11	12
13	14	15	16	17	18	19
20	21	22	23	24	25	26
27	28	29	30	31		

AUGUST
M	T	W	T	F	S	S
					1	2
3	4	5	6	7	8	9
10	11	12	13	14	15	16
17	18	19	20	21	22	23
24	25	26	27	28	29	30
31						

SEPTEMBER
M	T	W	T	F	S	S
	1	2	3	4	5	6
7	8	9	10	11	12	13
14	15	16	17	18	19	20
21	22	23	24	25	26	27
28	29	30				

OCTOBER
M	T	W	T	F	S	S
			1	2	3	4
5	6	7	8	9	10	11
12	13	14	15	16	17	18
19	20	21	22	23	24	25
26	27	28	29	30	31	

NOVEMBER
M	T	W	T	F	S	S
						1
2	3	4	5	6	7	8
9	10	11	12	13	14	15
16	17	18	19	20	21	22
23	24	25	26	27	28	29
30						

DECEMBER
M	T	W	T	F	S	S
1	2	3	4	5	6	
7	8	9	10	11	12	13
14	15	16	17	18	19	20
21	22	23	24	25	26	27
28	29	30	31			

GARDENS AND WILDLIFE

Gardens are an important ecosystem. All ecosystems are interdependent and dynamic systems of living organisms interacting with the physical environment. Gardens by their nature are extremely variable, with a diversity of plants that can surpass that of 'natural' ecosystems. Combined with resources such as ponds and compost heaps, gardens deliver a wide variety of habitats where wildlife can thrive. Gardens provide food and a home for thousands of creatures throughout their lifecycles, and this wildlife is vital to a healthy and vibrant living garden.

The large range of garden wildlife is there because of gardening, not despite it. Gardens provide resources year-round, from overwintering sites to summer food plants. No garden or green space is too small to provide some benefit. A window box, for instance, can provide a nectar stop for bumblebees and other pollinators. The huge range of plants and kinds of garden management results in a mosaic of habitats spanning a much wider area than a single garden. Wildlife doesn't recognise our boundaries in the way we do. Gardens, especially those with pervious perimeters such as hedges, provide important corridors enabling the movement of mammals such as hedgehogs, birds, butterflies and other creatures.

Most gardens already support a variety of wildlife and, with a little thought and planning, they can sustain even more. Adding more plants, a pond, bird, bee and bat boxes, decaying wood, a compost heap or an undisturbed leaf pile will provide valuable habitats. The more diverse the habitats, the greater the number of species and individuals of birds, bees, bats, beetles, moths and other animals that will use a garden. The RHS recognises and actively promotes the valuable contribution that wildlife makes to gardens and gardens to wildlife. The act of gardening for wildlife can also bring great enjoyment and health benefits to gardeners.

For more information visit: www.rhs.org.uk and www.wildaboutgardens.org

Female blackbird (*Turdus merula*)

PLANT FOR WILDLIFE

- Providing a wide range of habitats is the best way to encourage wildlife into your garden. Key features to consider including are trees, shrubs, lawn, flowers and water, such as a small pond.
- Hedges can provide important corridors for wildlife to move along safely, as well as nesting and hibernation sites.
- To provide a valuable food source for birds, consider planting more shrubs and trees that produce berries.
- Pruning your shrubs at different times will create varied cycles of growth and will benefit wildlife.
- A pile of logs can provide a micro-habitat to provide shelter for small animals and insects.
- Recycle garden waste in a compost heap; this will also provide a habitat for a wide range of insects and other invertebrates.

BIRDS

- Many natural sources of food such as seeds and berries are exhausted by this time of year, so it is more important than ever to feed the birds in your garden.
- You can make your own fat balls for birds using natural fats such as lard and beef suet (see week 9). Vegetable oil, fat from cooking and unsaturated margarines are not suitable. Alternatively, you can buy high-quality bird food online or from retail outlets.
- Clean bird tables and trays regularly. A simple bird tray is advisable, as complicated designs can be difficult to clean. Make sure it has a raised edge to retain food, and a gap in each corner to allow water to drain away and to help with cleaning.
- Make sure to move bird feeders around the garden regularly to avoid damaging the ground underneath and prevent droppings accumulating.
- Some common birds to see in the winter months are robins, blackbirds, thrushes (including redwings) and tits.

Providing a wide range of habitats is the best way to encourage wildlife into your garden

DECEMBER/JANUARY

Monday 30

Tuesday 31

New Year's Day
Holiday, UK, Republic of Ireland, USA, Canada,
Australia and New Zealand

Wednesday 01

Holiday, Scotland and New Zealand

Thursday 02

Friday 03

Saturday 04

Sunday 05

JANUARY

06 Monday

First quarter
Epiphany

07 Tuesday

08 Wednesday

09 Thursday

10 Friday

11 Saturday

12 Sunday

Rabbits (*Oryctolagus cuniculus*)

JANUARY

Full moon   Monday 13

Tuesday 14

Wednesday 15

Thursday 16

Friday 17

Saturday 18

Sunday 19

Nuthatch (*Sitta europaea*)

JANUARY

20 Monday

Martin Luther King Jnr Day
Holiday, USA

21 Tuesday

Last quarter

22 Wednesday

23 Thursday

24 Friday

25 Saturday

Burns Night

26 Sunday

Australia Day

Eurasian otter (*Lutra lutra*)

JOBS FOR THE MONTH

- A regular source of unfrozen water is essential for birds for drinking and bathing, so make sure to keep bird baths topped up and ice-free.
- To prevent diseases, clean bird baths and feeding stations regularly. It's also a good idea to avoid a build-up of spilt food, as this can encourage less desirable visitors such as rats.
- Move feeding stations around the garden to avoid an accumulation of spilt food as well as droppings.
- Position bird tables or feeders away from any areas easily accessed by cats, such a roofs, trees or fences. Placing your feeders next to prickly bushes can also be a good deterrent.
- Put up nestboxes for birds. These should be fitted with an entrance guard to protect them from predators and hung 1–3m high on walls or trees. Make sure any nestboxes face the north or east, and tilt the box forwards slightly to prevent rain from entering it.

PONDS

A pond provides an important water source for all wildlife, and even the smallest pond will attract dragonflies, damselflies and other insects, as well as newts, toads and frogs. If you put in a garden pond in late winter, you may even get your first frogs and toads by spring. Here are some tips for how to make your pond more wildlife-friendly:

- Connect your water butt to the pond so it will automatically fill during heavy rain.
- Try to vary the depth of the water to include shallow as well as deeper areas, as this variety will support more diverse wildlife.
- Choose a bright, sunny location with at least one sloping side to provide easy access in and out of the water.
- Create a safe passage for animals to enter and exit the pond by letting grass grow long or planting around the edges of the pond.
- It can be helpful to include a section with stones or gravel to provide easy drinking spots for pollinators such as bees.

A pond provides an important water source for all wildlife

JANUARY/FEBRUARY

Holiday, Australia (Australia Day)

Monday 27

Tuesday 28

New moon
Chinese New Year

Wednesday 29

Thursday 30

Friday 31

Saturday 01

Sunday 02

---

03 Monday

04 Tuesday

05 Wednesday   *First quarter*

06 Thursday   Waitangi Day
                                                           Holiday, New Zealand

07 Friday

08 Saturday

09 Sunday

Hawfinch (*Coccothraustes coccothraustes*)

FEBRUARY

Monday 10

Tuesday 11

Full moon   Wednesday 12

Thursday 13

Valentine's Day   Friday 14

Saturday 15

Sunday 16

Weasel (*Mustela nivalis*)

FEBRUARY

17 Monday

Presidents' Day
Holiday, USA

18 Tuesday

19 Wednesday

20 Thursday

Last quarter

21 Friday

22 Saturday

23 Sunday

Red Admiral (*Vanessa atalanta*)

JOBS FOR THE MONTH

- Scatter bird food on the ground and bird table. You can also hang bird feeders and fat balls on branches and fences, and keep them topped up. Birds follow a routine, so try to keep your feeding regime as consistent as possible to encourage birds to return regularly to the garden.
- It's a good idea to identify a suitable place in your garden to leave untouched as a wildlife area. Even a small untended patch behind a shed will be beneficial.
- Make improvements to your pond to make it more wildlife-friendly (see week 5). Look out for amphibian spawn in the pond: frog spawn is usually in jelly-like clumps; newt spawn is laid separately on pondweed stems; and toad spawn is in longer individual strands.
- Trim hedges and shrubs before bird nesting season begins.

MAKE FAT BALLS

You can easily make your own fat balls to feed birds in your garden. The colder months are an ideal time to make them.

1. Mix together one part natural fat (suet or lard work well) to two parts seeds, transfer to a saucepan and gently heat, stirring until the fat melts.
2. To make the balls, mould the seed mixture into balls using your hands. Space apart on a tray and place in the fridge to set for 24 hours.
3. Once the fat balls are solid, put out in the garden in a regular bird feeder or fat ball feeder.

Birds follow a routine, so keep your feeding regime as consistent as possible to encourage them to return to your garden

FEBRUARY/MARCH

Monday 24

Tuesday 25

Wednesday 26

Thursday 27

New moon   Friday 28

St David's Day   Saturday 01
First day of Ramadân (subject to sighting of the moon)

Sunday 02

MARCH

03 Monday

04 Tuesday   Shrove Tuesday

05 Wednesday   Ash Wednesday

06 Thursday   *First quarter*

07 Friday

08 Saturday

09 Sunday

Great tit (*Parus major*)

MARCH

Commonwealth Day   Monday 10

Tuesday 11

Wednesday 12

Thursday 13

Full moon   Friday 14

Saturday 15

Sunday 16

Red-headed cardinal beetle (*Pyrochroa serraticornis*)

17 Monday

St Patrick's Day
Holiday, Republic of Ireland and Northern Ireland

18 Tuesday

19 Wednesday

20 Thursday

Vernal Equinox (Spring begins)

21 Friday

22 Saturday

Last quarter

23 Sunday

Red squirrel (*Sciurus vulgaris*)

MARCH

Monday 24

Tuesday 25

Wednesday 26

Thursday 27

Friday 28

New moon   Saturday 29

British Summer Time begins   Sunday 30
Mothering Sunday, UK and Republic of Ireland
Eid al-Fitr (end of Ramadân) (subject to sighting of the moon)

Common frog (*Rana temporaria*)

MARCH/APRIL

31 Monday

01 Tuesday

02 Wednesday

03 Thursday

04 Friday

05 Saturday   *First quarter*

06 Sunday

BIRDS

By this time of the year, nesting season is well underway and migrant birds such as willow warblers, swifts, house martins and swallows will be arriving from Africa. The dawn chorus can be deafening as birds compete with each other for territories and mates. You may see swallows or spotted flycatchers nesting on quiet outbuildings or suitable ledges.

CHOOSING BIRD FOOD

Leaving out food particular to a bird's requirements will encourage that species of bird into your garden.

- Tits: insect cakes
- Finches: berry cakes
- Robins: live mealworms
- Sparrows, finches and nuthatches: sunflower heads
- Goldfinches: niger seeds
- Wrens: prefer natural foods but will take fat and seeds
- Starlings: peanut cakes
- Dunnocks: fat and small seeds on the ground
- Thrushes and blackbirds: fruit such as raisins, over-ripe apples and songbird mix scattered on the ground.

JOBS FOR THE MONTH

- Continue to top up bird feeders. Whole peanuts should be placed in a metal mesh feeder as they can be a choking hazard for fledglings.
- Plant a hanging basket or window box somewhere sunny to attract bees and butterflies using nasturtiums, English marigolds and lavender.
- Make or buy a bat box and mount it on a sheltered but sunny wall.
- Plant annuals and perennials (single flowers as opposed to double flowers) to encourage pollinators into the garden. You can find examples of these on the RHS Plants for Pollinators lists.

Nesting season is well underway

APRIL

Monday 07

Tuesday 08

Wednesday 09

Thursday 10

Friday 11

Saturday 12

Full moon
Palm Sunday
First day of Passover (Pesach)

Sunday 13

Harvest mouse (*Micromys minutus*)

APRIL

14 Monday

15 Tuesday

16 Wednesday

17 Thursday

Maundy Thursday

18 Friday

Good Friday
Holiday, UK, Canada, Australia and New Zealand

19 Saturday

20 Sunday

Easter Sunday

Common blue (*Polyommatus icarus*)

APRIL

Last quarter
Easter Monday
Holiday, UK (exc. Scotland), Republic of Ireland,
Australia and New Zealand

Monday 21

Earth Day

Tuesday 22

St George's Day

Wednesday 23

Thursday 24

Anzac Day
Holiday, Australia and New Zealand

Friday 25

Saturday 26

New moon

Sunday 27

Juvenile robin (*Erithacus rubecula*)

APRIL/MAY

28 Monday

29 Tuesday

30 Wednesday

01 Thursday

02 Friday

03 Saturday

04 Sunday

First quarter

JOBS FOR THE MONTH

- Leave out food and water for hedgehogs, providing fuel as they come out of hibernation.
- Remove excess plant growth from ponds. Make sure to leave this out for twenty-four hours before adding it to the compost heap, to allow any trapped creatures to return to the water.
- Stop mowing an area of lawn to allow the grass and flowers to grow. This will attract all sorts of grasshoppers, bugs, ground-nesting bees and other insects.
- Keep the bird bath and feeders clean and topped up. Put out additional food on the ground, making sure to avoid chunky foods that might cause young fledglings to choke.
- Leave informal hedges untrimmed to provide food and shelter for wildlife. Never cut a hedge or shrub if you suspect nesting birds are present.
- Clean out solitary bee hotels and any hedgehog houses if you have them in your garden.

ENCOURAGE INSECTS INTO THE GARDEN

Insects and other invertebrates are crucial to your garden's natural balance. They help to break down dead plant matter and are vital for nutrient recycling. Many flying insects are also pollinators. Here are some tips for encouraging insects into your garden:

- Create log, twig and rock piles to provide protection and create shelter for insects.
- Ladybirds, spiders and other insects find winter shelter in evergreen bushes and climbers, and among fallen leaves, dead stems and seedheads.
- A compost heap for recycling garden waste will also provide a habitat for many insects.
- Mulch beds with garden compost to help feed earthworms and maintain a healthy living soil.
- Avoid using herbicides and make sure to weed by hand as much as possible. Weeds can be a valuable source of nectar and pollen, so try to leave some weeds in lawns.

Log, twig and rock piles provide protection and create shelter for insects

Early Spring Bank Holiday, UK
Holiday, Republic of Ireland

Monday 05

Coronation Day

Tuesday 06

Wednesday 07

Thursday 08

Friday 09

Saturday 10

Mother's Day, USA, Canada, Australia
and New Zealand

Sunday 11

Large skipper (*Ochlodes sylvanus*)

MAY

12 Monday

Full moon

13 Tuesday

14 Wednesday

15 Thursday

16 Friday

17 Saturday

18 Sunday

Honey bee (*Apis mellifera*)

MAY

Victoria Day
Holiday, Canada

Monday 19

Last quarter

Tuesday 20

Wednesday 21

Thursday 22

Friday 23

Saturday 24

Sunday 25

European badger (*Meles meles*)

MAY/JUNE

---

26 Monday

Spring Bank Holiday, UK
Memorial Day
Holiday, USA

---

27 Tuesday

New moon

---

28 Wednesday

---

29 Thursday

Ascension Day

---

30 Friday

---

31 Saturday

---

01 Sunday

MAKE AN UPCYCLED CONTAINER POND

You can make a wildlife-friendly container pond by upcycling an old plastic container.

- Fill your container with rainwater. If the container leaks, you can use a sheet of pond liner to make it watertight, securing it in place with a silicone-based sealer.
- Gently lower in a mix of floating and upright pond plants. For a mini-pond, three to five plants is usually enough. They may look small to start with, but they can grow very quickly.
- Creating a ramp to your container pond will mean that frogs and other wildlife can get in and out. A stack of stones, bricks or logs can all work well.
- Make sure to position your container somewhere that catches a little sun, but where it won't be in the sun all day as this can warm the water up too much or cause it to evaporate too quickly.

SPIDERS

Spiders have an important role to play in an ecologically balanced garden. As well as eating insects, they are part of the food chain and provide a food source for birds. To encourage spiders, try to use pesticides as little as possible and plant tall flowers and dense bushes to create 'scaffolding' for spiders to build their webs on. Leave some bare soil for hunting spiders to catch prey and allow a patch of lawn to grow long as a home for nursery spiders.

HEDGEHOGS

Hedgehogs are very active at this time of year, with litters usually being born in June or July. Young mammals are beginning to explore the world beyond their homes, and you may see or hear their parents foraging for food at night.

Hedgehogs are active at this time of year

Feast of Weeks (Shavuot)
Holiday, Republic of Ireland
Holiday, New Zealand (The King's Birthday)

Monday 02

First quarter

Tuesday 03

Wednesday 04

Thursday 05

Friday 06

First day of Eid al-Adha

Saturday 07

Whit Sunday

Sunday 08

Ruddy darter dragonfly (*Sympetrum sanguineum*)

JUNE

09 Monday   Holiday, Australia (The King's Birthday)

10 Tuesday

11 Wednesday   *Full moon*

12 Thursday

13 Friday

14 Saturday   The King's Official Birthday (subject to confirmation)

15 Sunday   Father's Day, UK, Republic of Ireland, USA and Canada
Trinity Sunday

Common dormouse (*Muscardinus avellanarius*)

JUNE

Monday 16

Tuesday 17

Last quarter   Wednesday 18

Juneteenth   Thursday 19
Holiday, USA
Corpus Christi

Holiday, New Zealand (Matariki)   Friday 20

Summer solstice (Summer begins)   Saturday 21

Sunday 22

Marsh fritillary (*Euphydryas aurinia*)

JUNE

---

23 Monday

---

24 Tuesday

---

25 Wednesday   *New moon*

---

26 Thursday

---

27 Friday   Islamic New Year

---

28 Saturday

---

29 Sunday

Common lizard (*Zootoca vivipara*)

JOBS FOR THE MONTH

- Construct a hedgehog feeding station for the garden, making sure to put out hedgehog food and water regularly, particularly when it is very dry. You should also check that holes in the bottom of fences haven't become blocked, so hedgehogs can move freely between gardens.
- Avoid pruning hip-producing roses – these are a valuable source of food for wildlife.
- Allow your lawn to grow longer, letting some lawn flowers bloom.
- Delay hedge trimming until the end of summer to allow wildlife to nest, shelter and feed in them. You should also leave fledglings undisturbed if you find them on the ground – their parents are probably not far away.
- Use stored rainwater to top up ponds and water features if necessary. Tadpoles are developing their hind legs and will be emerging from the water to seek shelter among marginal pond plants; they are very vulnerable to predators at this time of year.

INSECTS

You can find lots of insects in the garden at this time of year.

- There is an abundance of hoverflies in the garden now. Adult hoverflies are pollinators and the larvae of many species feed on greenfly and other aphids.
- Summer is flying ant season, so look out for these.
- Wasps are useful flower pollinators and can also be good pest controllers.
- Growing herbs such as marjoram, mint and sage is a great way to encourage butterflies and bees to your garden.
- Avoid the use of lawn weedkillers to allow insect life to thrive.
- Try making a bee drinking station out of a plant saucer filled with pebbles and water.

Allow your lawn to grow longer,
letting some lawn flowers bloom

JUNE/JULY

Monday 30

Canada Day
Holiday, Canada

Tuesday 01

First quarter

Wednesday 02

Thursday 03

Independence Day
Holiday, USA

Friday 04

Saturday 05

Sunday 06

JULY

07 Monday

08 Tuesday

09 Wednesday

10 Thursday   *Full moon*

11 Friday

12 Saturday   Battle of the Boyne

13 Sunday

Red Admiral caterpillar (*Vanessa atalanta*)

JULY

Holiday, Northern Ireland (Battle of the Boyne) — **Monday 14**

St Swithin's Day — **Tuesday 15**

Wednesday 16

Thursday 17

Last quarter — **Friday 18**

Saturday 19

Sunday 20

Starling (*Sturnus vulgaris*)

JULY

21 Monday

22 Tuesday

23 Wednesday

24 Thursday   *New moon*

25 Friday

26 Saturday

27 Sunday

Black arches moth (*Lymantria monacha*)

IN THE GARDEN

- Many adult birds are fairly secretive in late summer, hiding in cool, shady places in the garden while their feathers are replaced during the summer moult.
- Birdsong may be reduced or less obvious this month, and young birds can be seen exploring their environment. In hot, dry weather many birds enjoy 'dust-bathing' as well as washing in the bird bath.
- Squirrels can be heard chattering and squealing at one another while chasing each other around the treetops.
- August sees the departure of swifts, although the majority of other migrant bird species can still be found in the garden. Starlings, jackdaws and house sparrows, in particular, can be seen caring for their young in their nests.
- In late summer, butterflies like Red Admiral and Painted Lady will appreciate fallen fruit left on the ground. They are also particularly attracted to buddleja.
- Bumblebees, solitary bees and hoverflies are busy collecting nectar and pollen from flowers and herb gardens.

BUTTERFLIES

Some of the most common butterflies to see in the garden are Red Admiral, Painted Lady, Comma, Brimstone, Peacock, Green-veined White, Small White and Large White. The Small Tortoiseshell used to be seen commonly but its numbers have declined in recent years. To encourage butterflies to your garden, make sure to plant a range of nectar-rich flowers such as red valerian and asters. To support butterflies, you also need to look after the caterpillars in your garden, so research which plants will best support them.

To encourage butterflies to your garden, plant a range of nectar-rich flowers

JULY/AUGUST

Monday 28

Tuesday 29

Wednesday 30

Thursday 31

First quarter

Friday 01

Saturday 02

Sunday 03

AUGUST

04 Monday   Holiday, Scotland and Republic of Ireland

05 Tuesday

06 Wednesday

07 Thursday

08 Friday

09 Saturday   *Full moon*

10 Sunday

Eurasian siskin (*Spinus spinus*)

AUGUST

Monday 11

Tuesday 12

Wednesday 13

Thursday 14

Friday 15

Last quarter

Saturday 16

Sunday 17

Hoverfly (*Syrphidae*)

AUGUST

18 Monday

19 Tuesday

20 Wednesday

21 Thursday

22 Friday

23 Saturday   *New moon*

24 Sunday

AUGUST

Summer Bank Holiday, UK (exc. Scotland)   Monday 25

Tuesday 26

Wednesday 27

Thursday 28

Friday 29

Saturday 30

First quarter   Sunday 31

Emperor dragonfly (*Anax imperator*)

SEPTEMBER

01 Monday

Holiday, USA (Labor Day)
Holiday, Canada (Labour Day)

02 Tuesday

03 Wednesday

04 Thursday

05 Friday

06 Saturday

07 Sunday

Full moon
Father's Day, Australia and New Zealand

BATS

- Bats are excellent pest controllers. All bats are legally protected in Britain and this also extends to their roosting, breeding and hibernation sites.
- There are 17 species of bat breeding in Britain; the more common species to see in the garden are the common and soprano pipistrelle, brown long-eared, noctule and Daubenton's.
- Bats eat flying insects at night, including mosquitoes, moths and beetles, helping to keep garden pests at bay. Late summer is the best time for bat watching in the evening.
- Garden ponds and night-flowering plants such as evening primrose encourage the types of insects that bats like to hunt.
- During the day bats hide in dark places like hollow trees, so retain old trees with cavities in the trunk, where possible.

JOBS FOR THE MONTH

- Deadhead flowers to encourage them to produce more blooms and pollen for insects.
- Give meadows a final cut before winter. Leave the clippings to lie for a couple of days before removing. This will allow wildflower seeds to fall to the ground and replenish the meadow.
- Cover the pond surface with netting to stop excessive amounts of fallen leaves from getting in.
- As we come to the end of the nesting season, hedge trimming can resume – however, delay for another month if you suspect birds are still active.
- Continue to clean and top up bird feeders and put food on bird tables and on the ground. Leave some windfall apples, pears and plums for birds to feed on.
- Allow seedheads to develop on some plants as a food source. Don't trim any bushes with developing berries, such as holly, cotoneaster and pyracantha.
- Remove dead foliage and blooms from aquatic plants. Leave at the side of the pond for a while to allow wildlife to return to the water before adding them to the compost heap.

Top up bird feeders and put food on bird tables and on the ground

SEPTEMBER

Accession of King Charles III   Monday 08

Tuesday 09

Wednesday 10

Thursday 11

Friday 12

Saturday 13

Last quarter   Sunday 14

Goldcrest (*Regulus regulus*)

SEPTEMBER

15 Monday

16 Tuesday

17 Wednesday

18 Thursday

19 Friday

20 Saturday

21 Sunday

New moon

European hedgehog (*Erinaceus europaeus*)

SEPTEMBER

Autumnal Equinox (Autumn begins)

Monday 22

Jewish New Year (Rosh Hashanah)

Tuesday 23

Wednesday 24

Thursday 25

Friday 26

Saturday 27

Sunday 28

Small tortoiseshell (*Aglais urticae*)

29 Monday

First quarter
Michaelmas Day

30 Tuesday

01 Wednesday

02 Thursday

Day of Atonement (Yom Kippur)

03 Friday

04 Saturday

05 Sunday

PREPARE FOR WINTER

Help hibernating creatures survive the cold weather by making hibernation places in your garden, such as creating a log pile for beetles, making a 'bug hotel' out of hollow stems and building a hedgehog box. Even a pile of old leaves left undisturbed will provide a home for small mammals and many insects.

MAMMALS

Foxes may become more inquisitive as natural food sources become scarce, so always secure your bins. This is mating season for bats and they will be building up fat reserves to survive the coming winter. Other mammals also start going into hibernation. During mild spells, hedgehogs can emerge to forage for food, before returning to their hiding places as the temperature drops. Give them special hedgehog food, or dog or cat food, but never bread and milk. Only leave food out during the winter months if it is being taken, but continue to provide a source of clean, fresh water and be careful that it doesn't freeze over.

JOBS FOR THE MONTH

- If possible, allow uncut ivy to flower as it is an excellent late nectar source for pollinating insects and the berries last well into winter to feed birds.
- Be careful when turning over compost heaps, as frogs, toads and other small animals may be sheltering there.
- Avoid disturbing butterflies such as Red Admirals, which overwinter in garden buildings.
- Autumn daisies are a good source of food for butterflies and bees, particularly when there are few other plants for them to feed on.
- Clean the bird bath regularly and ensure that it is filled with fresh water. Keep feeding stations clean and topped up.
- Leave herbaceous and hollow-stemmed plants unpruned until early spring to provide homes for overwintering insects.
- Where possible, leave seedheads standing to provide food and shelter for wildlife.

Leave seedheads standing to provide food and shelter for wildlife

OCTOBER

Monday 06

Full moon
First day of Tabernacles (Succoth)

Tuesday 07

Wednesday 08

Thursday 09

Friday 10

Saturday 11

Sunday 12

Great spotted woodpecker (*Dendrocopos major*)

OCTOBER

13 Monday

14 Tuesday

15 Wednesday

16 Thursday

17 Friday

18 Saturday

19 Sunday

7-spot ladybird (*Coccinella septempunctata*)

OCTOBER

Monday 20

New moon

Tuesday 21

Wednesday 22

Thursday 23

Friday 24

Saturday 25

British Summer Time ends

Sunday 26

Common vole (*Microtus arvalis*)

OCTOBER/NOVEMBER

27 Monday

Holiday, Republic of Ireland
Holiday, New Zealand (Labour Day)

28 Tuesday

29 Wednesday

First quarter

30 Thursday

31 Friday

Halloween

01 Saturday

All Saints' Day

02 Sunday

MOTHS

- There are over 2,500 species of moths in Britain, which play an important role in garden ecosystems.
- Adult moths and their caterpillars are a key food source for various animals including hedgehogs, spiders, frogs, bats and birds. Day-flying and night-flying moths act as plant pollinators.
- To encourage more moths into your garden, leave longer grasses, knapweeds and thistles in the garden, and leave hedges untrimmed if possible. Tolerate caterpillar feeding damage to plants.
- Planting evergreen shrubs will provide overwintering sites for butterflies and moths.
- Planting birch, hornbeam, hawthorn, lady's bedstraw, willow and rowan will help support moth caterpillars.
- Planting common jasmine, sweet rocket, lychnis and sea lavender attracts day-flying moths and many other pollinators.
- Night-flowering, nectar-rich plants such as night-scented stock and pale-coloured flowering plants attract nocturnal moths.

JOBS FOR THE MONTH

- Animals still need access to water for drinking, so melt a hole in ice at the edge of a pond by filling a saucepan with hot water and placing it on the ice until a hole has melted. Never crack or hit the ice, as the shockwaves created can harm nearby wildlife.
- Empty and clean out bird nestboxes using boiling water. When they are thoroughly dry, place a handful of wood shavings inside to provide winter shelter.
- Consider options other than a bonfire for disposing of garden waste. If you do have a bonfire, always check for animals before lighting it.
- Make a leaf pile for overwintering mammals and retain fallen leaves at the base of hedges for blackbirds and thrushes to hunt through for invertebrates.
- Now is the time to make sure you are putting out high-fat foods for birds to eat, such as peanut cakes and fat balls (see week 9). Wrens and other small birds appreciate finely chopped bacon rind and grated cheese.

Empty and clean out nestboxes

NOVEMBER

Monday 03

Tuesday 04

Full moon
Guy Fawkes Night

Wednesday 05

Thursday 06

Friday 07

Saturday 08

Remembrance Sunday

Sunday 09

House sparrow (*Passer domesticus*)

NOVEMBER

10 Monday

11 Tuesday

Holiday, USA (Veterans Day)
Holiday, Canada (Remembrance Day)

12 Wednesday

Last quarter

13 Thursday

14 Friday

Birthday of King Charles III

15 Saturday

16 Sunday

Meadow grasshopper (*Chorthippus parallelus*)

NOVEMBER

Monday 17

Tuesday 18

Wednesday 19

New moon   Thursday 20

Friday 21

Saturday 22

Sunday 23

Ivy mining bee (*Colletes hederae*)

24 Monday

25 Tuesday

26 Wednesday

27 Thursday — Holiday, USA (Thanksgiving)

28 Friday — *First quarter*

29 Saturday

30 Sunday — St Andrew's Day
First Sunday in Advent

Chiffchaff (*Phylloscopus collybita*)

JOBS FOR THE MONTH

- Mulch vegetable beds with garden compost but delay cutting back borders until late winter, to provide shelter for invertebrates.
- Keep the bird bath topped up, clean and ice-free.
- Take care when pruning, as butterflies and moths overwinter in places that are sheltered from wind, frost and rain. They favour a thick tangle of leaves and stems, but some will use sheds or garages.
- Make sure to put out food for birds regularly, so they don't waste vital energy on visiting when there's no food.
- Plant hedges, single-flowered roses and fruit trees to offer plenty of resources for wildlife, including blossom and fruit.
- Encourage newts to breed by introducing some non-invasive, submerged, aquatic plants into your pond. Newts lay their eggs on narrow-leaved plants in the spring.

CHRISTMAS DECORATIONS

Holly berries are a valuable food source for birds, so think twice before using them in any Christmas decorations. You can make a wildlife-friendly Christmas wreath for your front door out of garden moss, holly leaves and ivy. You can also use spruce, pine, birch, willow or dogwood, and decorate it with rosehips.

Hedges, single-flowered roses and fruit trees all offer resources for wildlife

DECEMBER

Holiday, Scotland (St Andrew's Day)

Monday 01

Tuesday 02

Wednesday 03

Full moon

Thursday 04

Friday 05

Saturday 06

Sunday 07

DECEMBER

08 Monday

09 Tuesday

10 Wednesday

11 Thursday   *Last quarter*

12 Friday

13 Saturday

14 Sunday   Hanukkah begins (at sunset)

Tawny owls (*Strix aluco*)

DECEMBER

Monday 15

Tuesday 16

Wednesday 17

Thursday 18

Friday 19

New moon

Saturday 20

Winter Solstice (Winter begins)

Sunday 21

Dew drops on spider web

DECEMBER

22 Monday

Hanukkah ends

23 Tuesday

24 Wednesday

Christmas Eve

25 Thursday

Christmas Day
Holiday, UK, Republic of Ireland, USA, Canada,
Australia and New Zealand

26 Friday

Boxing Day (St Stephen's Day)
Holiday, UK, Republic of Ireland, USA, Canada,
Australia and New Zealand

27 Saturday

First quarter

28 Sunday

Red fox (*Vulpes vulpes*)

DECEMBER/JANUARY

Monday 29

Tuesday 30

New Year's Eve

Wednesday 31

New Year's Day
Holiday, UK, Republic of Ireland, USA, Canada,
Australia and New Zealand

Thursday 01

Holiday, Scotland and New Zealand

Friday 02

Saturday 03

Sunday 04

Goldfinch (*Carduelis carduelis*)

YEAR PLANNER

January	July
February	**August**
March	**September**
April	**October**
May	**November**
June	**December**